livehappy™

© 2014 Live Happy LLC
Published by Live Happy LLC.

LIVE HAPPY LLC
4006 Belt Line Road Ste. 120
Addison, Texas 75001
USA
www.livehappy.com

Editor in Chief: Karol DeWulf Nickell
Art Director: Kathryn Finney
Copy and Assistant Managing Editor: Whitney Alswede
Cover and Book Designer: Wendy Johnson
Copy Editor: Betsy Simnacher
Illustrations: Susy Pilgrim Waters

Printed in the United States of America

ISBN-10: 0692297073
ISBN-13: 978-0-692-29707-0

livehappy™

50 happiness facts & quotes

table of contents

Welcome to Happiness

HAPPINESS IS THE PERFECT GIFT.

It fits all sizes, ages, and kinds of people. Everyone wants it, so there are no returns. It has no expiration date and never goes out of style. Happiness is the gift that keeps on giving. It has a proven residual effect. Happiness inspires other positive emotions, like love, compassion, gratitude, and generosity. And, thank goodness, wrapping isn't necessary.

HOW MUCH DO YOU KNOW ABOUT HAPPINESS?

Research from happiness experts Ed Diener, Ph.D.; Sonja Lyubomirsky, Ph.D.; and Laura King, Ph.D., shows that happier people are more likely to have:

- better health and longer lives
- more fulfilling marriages and relationships
- higher incomes and more financial success
- better work performance and more professional success
- more altruism and social and community involvement

With all these benefits, it's clear why more people want to learn how to be happier.

THAT'S WHERE LIVE HAPPY COMES IN.

At Live Happy, we are leading a global movement to make the world a happier place. Through content, events, tools, and products that reflect our holistic approach to happiness, we seek to inspire, engage, and inform the seekers, achievers, givers, and compassionates of the world.

THIS BOOK, THE FIRST FROM LIVE HAPPY, IS OUR GIFT TO YOU.

It is our selection of more than 50 facts and quotes about happiness that you can refer to every day at home, work, and play. It is also the perfect book to share with others.

HAPPINESS IS THE PERFECT GIFT— PASS IT ON!

RELATIONSHIPS—ESPECIALLY WITH OUR FAMILY AND FRIENDS—are one of the largest pillars upon which our happiness is built. And when we foster them, when we invest ourselves and our time, we receive the ultimate gifts: love and long-lasting happiness.

But the connection between love, happiness, and relationships isn't a one-way street; it's actually quite the opposite. Live Happy's experts have found that when we feel loved and are happy, our relationships tend to be more fulfilling, and our happiness becomes contagious.

So, take time out for the people who matter and deepen your relationships—it's the best decision you'll ever make.

WHEN WE'RE IN LOVE WITH SOMEONE, WE MIRROR HIS OR HER FEELINGS, GOALS, AND EVEN MEMORIES.

SOURCE: *THE NEW SCIENCE OF LOVE: HOW UNDERSTANDING YOUR BRAIN'S WIRING CAN HELP REKINDLE YOUR RELATIONSHIP*

WHEN RESEARCH SUBJECTS WERE ASKED, "WHY GET MARRIED?" they said **"love"** most often, with 88 percent citing it as a **"very important reason,"** followed by **"making a lifelong commitment"** (81 percent), **"companionship"** (76 percent), and **"having children"** (49 percent).

SOURCE: PEW RESEARCH

"Being deeply loved by someone gives you strength, while loving someone deeply gives you courage."

—Lao Tzu

"I have decided to stick with love. Hate is too great a burden to bear." —Martin Luther King Jr.

"The love of family and the admiration of friends is much more important than wealth and privilege." —*Charles Kuralt*

IN A STUDY OF NEARLY
300 MEN OVER THE COURSE
OF 75 YEARS, HAVING
STRONG RELATIONSHIPS
WAS FOUND TO BE THE
BIGGEST PREDICTOR OF
LIFE SATISFACTION AND
THE ONLY THING THAT
TRULY MATTERS.

SOURCE: THE HARVARD GRANT STUDY

"We feel happiest when we are growing in our relationships or our ability to change the world for the positive (optimism) or when we see life as a challenge instead of a threat." —*Shawn Achor*

"Ancient philosophers and contemporary scientists agree that relationships are a key, and maybe the key, to happiness. So certainly people who have more relationships and deeper relationships are happier."

—*Gretchen Rubin*

"*Love is a flower—*
you've got to let it grow."

—John Lennon

"Love, from your body's perspective, is a biological wave of good feeling and mutual care that rolls through two or more brains and bodies at once. Your body needs these micromoments of positivity resonance just like it needs good food and physical activity....The more of these micromoments you each have, the more each of you grows happier, healthier, and wiser."

—*Barbara Fredrickson, Ph.D.*

When men marry, their risk of death decreases, thanks in part to their wives' support and social connections.

SOURCE: "THE EFFECTS OF MARRIAGE ON HEALTH:
A SYNTHESIS OF RECENT RESEARCH EVIDENCE"

Creativity

WHETHER WE REALIZE IT OR NOT, WE'RE ALL CREATIVE. We may not be the next Picasso, Julia Child, or Elvis, but when there's a problem to be solved, whether it's stopping a child's cries or working the budget numbers, our ingenuity kicks in and our creativity takes the wheel.

And with those creative juices, inevitably, positive feelings follow. Our everyday creativity is what paints a black-and-white world with splashes of magenta, cerulean, and emerald. And it's what turns an average, ho-hum day into one filled with smiles, laughter, and happiness.

Go. Release your creative self. When you do, you will discover a richer, more enchanting life awaits.

IF YOU'RE HAPPY AND YOU KNOW IT…IT'S EASIER TO BE CREATIVE. RESEARCH SHOWS THAT WHEN WE'RE HAPPY, OUR AMYGDALAS—THE PART OF THE BRAIN THAT CAN INHIBIT CREATIVITY—BECOME QUIET, ALLOWING US TO APPROACH PROBLEMS MORE CREATIVELY.

SOURCE: "POSITIVE AFFECT INCREASES THE BREADTH OF ATTENTIONAL SELECTION"

"This world is but a canvas

"Life is too short to be in a hurry. If we are always on the go, we are reacting to the exigencies of day-to-day life rather than allowing ourselves the space to create a happy life."

—*Tal Ben-Shahar, Ph.D., in* Happier: Learn the Secrets to Daily Joy and Lasting Fulfillment

Listening to POSITIVE, UPBEAT tunes can improve our moods—if we tell ourselves it will. And once the MUSIC IS PLAYING, make an effort to actively listen to it to really reap the most MOOD-BOOSTING BENEFITS.

SOURCE: "TRYING TO BE HAPPIER REALLY CAN WORK: TWO EXPERIMENTAL STUDIES"

"Think left and think right and think low and think high. Oh, the thinks you *can* think up if only you try."

—Dr. Seuss

ONE STUDY OF 79 STUDENTS
FOUND THAT THE ONES WHO
DESCRIBED THEMSELVES AS
HAPPY AND ACTIVE WERE MORE
LIKELY TO BE PARTICIPATING IN A
CREATIVE PURSUIT, NO MATTER
HOW "FRIVOLOUS, AMATEURISH,
OR WEIRD" IT WAS.

SOURCE: "EVERYDAY CREATIVITY IN DAILY LIFE:
AN EXPERIENCE-SAMPLING STUDY OF 'LITTLE C' CREATIVITY"

"There is a fountain of youth: It is your mind, your talents, the creativity you bring to your life and the lives of people you love. When you learn to tap this source, you will truly have defeated age." —*Sophia Loren*

WHEN EMPLOYEES ARE HAPPY, THEY ARE MORE LIKELY TO BE PRODUCTIVE AND COME UP WITH NEW IDEAS.

SOURCE: *THE PROGRESS PRINCIPLE*

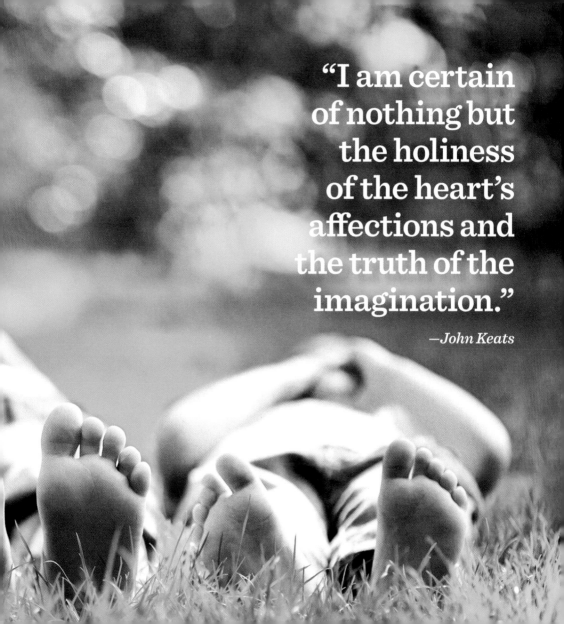

"I am certain of nothing but the holiness of the heart's affections and the truth of the imagination."

—*John Keats*

"The idea is not to live forever; it is to create something that will."

—Andy Warhol

FOR A CREATIVE BOOST, TURN TO BLUE. RESEARCH SHOWS THAT SURROUNDING OURSELVES WITH BLUE CAN HELP US THINK MORE CREATIVELY.

SOURCE: "BLUE OR RED? EXPLORING THE EFFECT OF COLOR ON COGNITIVE TASK PERFORMANCES"

LOOKING FOR A CREATIVITY BOOST? TAKE A HIKE!

A brisk walk can increase your creative thinking by as much as 60 percent.

SOURCE: "GIVE YOUR IDEAS SOME LEGS: THE POSITIVE EFFECT OF WALKING ON CREATIVE THINKING"

"Passion is one great force that unleashes creativity, because if you're passionate about something, then you're more willing to take risks."

—Yo-Yo Ma

THERE IS PERHAPS NO SIMPLER PATH TO
HAPPINESS THAN EXPRESSING GRATITUDE—
for friends who always lend an ear, the warmth of a
sweater, new opportunities, for what life has brought us.

When we make this act of "thanksgiving" part of our
daily lives, our mood is lighter, we're better prepared to
handle challenges, we have more satisfying relationships,
we're happier, we're more enthusiastic—people even
perceive and treat us differently.

In short, expressions of gratitude are simple acts that
create mountains of results.

So, join us as we celebrate gratitude and celebrate all
that we have to be thankful for, each and every day.

"When we give cheerfully and accept gratefully, everyone is blessed." —*Maya Angelou*

When it comes to expressing gratitude at home, men take the win, with 67 percent saying they express their gratitude to their spouses daily, while only 59 percent of women follow suit.

SOURCE: GRATITUDE SURVEY CONDUCTED FOR THE JOHN TEMPLETON FOUNDATION

ONLY 10 PERCENT OF US EXPRESS THANKS OR APPRECIATION TO OUR COLLEAGUES ON A DAILY BASIS—EVEN THOUGH SAYING "THANK YOU" TO A CO-WORKER MAKES US FEEL HAPPIER AND MORE MOTIVATED.

SOURCE: GRATITUDE SURVEY CONDUCTED FOR THE JOHN TEMPLETON FOUNDATION

Of three test groups, the one asked to focus on gratitude was 25 percent happier, was more optimistic, and even exercised an hour and a half longer than its peers in the other two groups.

SOURCE: STUDY BY ROBERT EMMONS, PH.D., FOR *THANKS!*

"As we express our gratitude, we must never forget that the highest appreciation is not to utter words, but to live by them." —*John F. Kennedy*

IN A SURVEY OF 3,000 AMERICANS, RESEARCHERS WITNESSED AN IMMEDIATE RUSH OF FEELINGS OF GRATITUDE AFTER SEPT. 11. THE REASON? THE INCREASED SENSE OF BELONGING THAT RESULTED FROM THE TRAGEDY.

SOURCE: "CHARACTER STRENGTHS BEFORE AND AFTER SEPTEMBER 11"

"Having gratitude and not expressing it is like wrapping a present and not giving it." —William Arthur Ward

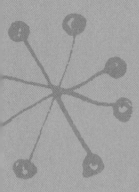

NINETY PERCENT OF SURVEY RESPONDENTS SAID THEY WERE GRATEFUL FOR THEIR FAMILIES, BUT ONLY 76 PERCENT SHARED THEIR GRATITUDE WITH THEIR CHILDREN, AND EVEN FEWER, 49 PERCENT, TOLD THEIR PARENTS.

SOURCE: GRATITUDE SURVEY CONDUCTED FOR THE JOHN TEMPLETON FOUNDATION

ONE STUDY FOUND
THAT WHEN WE EXPRESS
GRATITUDE FOR SOMEONE
HELPING US, THE HELPER
IS MORE LIKELY TO FEEL
VALUED—AND MORE THAN
DOUBLED THE LIKELIHOOD
THAT HE OR SHE WOULD HELP
OTHER PEOPLE.

SOURCE: "A LITTLE THANKS GOES A LONG WAY: EXPLAINING
WHY GRATITUDE EXPRESSIONS MOTIVATE PROSOCIAL BEHAVIOR"

"I feel a very unusual sensation—
if it is not indigestion, I think it
must be gratitude." —*Benjamin Disraeli*

"When you are grateful—
when you can see what you
have—you unlock blessings
to flow in your life." —Suze Orman

"At the age of 18, I made up my mind to never have another bad day in my life. I dove into an endless sea of gratitude from which I've never emerged."

—*Patch Adams*

"Gratitude is many things to many people. It is wonder; it is appreciation; it is looking at the bright side of a setback; it is fathoming abundance; it is thanking someone in your life; it is thanking God; it is 'counting blessings.' It is savoring; it is not taking things for granted; it is coping; it is present-oriented."

—*Sonja Lyubomirsky in* The How of Happiness

RELIGION SEEMS TO POSITIVELY AFFECT OUR GRATITUDE. IN ONE SURVEY, 75 PERCENT OF THE MOST RELIGIOUS RESPONDENTS AGREED WITH THE STATEMENT "I HAVE SO MUCH IN LIFE TO BE THANKFUL FOR," WHEREAS ONLY 39 PERCENT OF THOSE CONSIDERED NON-RELIGIOUS AGREED.

SOURCE: GRATITUDE SURVEY CONDUCTED FOR THE JOHN TEMPLETON FOUNDATION

PEOPLE WHO MAKE
EXPRESSING GRATITUDE
A PART OF THEIR
LIVES SAY THEY SLEEP
LONGER (AND BETTER),
ARE OUTGOING, ARE
OPTIMISTIC, TAKE BETTER
CARE OF THEIR HEALTH,
AND FEEL MORE ALIVE.

SOURCE: ROBERT EMMONS, PH.D.

purpose

IT'S A FACT: WE'RE WIRED TO HELP OTHERS.

It makes sense then that we gain the most happiness not when we purchase a new phone or pair of designer shoes, but when we make contributions to further the greater good, when we pursue something in life that's bigger than us and makes a real contribution to society.

Whether it's teaching inner-city children, traveling across the globe to help those in need, or even organizing a donation drive at home, we at Live Happy believe pursuing our purpose is not only a birthright— it's necessary to our happiness.

"Those who have failed to work toward the truth have missed the purpose of living." —Gautama Buddha

"Studies show that people who help others without expecting anything in return feel better about themselves. Think of how great the world would be if everyone did one thing to help someone else. Collectively, our commitment to happiness can change the world." —*Jeff Olson*

"The meaning of life is life."
—*Alan Alda*

WHILE ONLY
1 PERCENT OF
EMPLOYEES SAY
THEY LOVE THEIR
JOBS, NEARLY
EVERYONE WHO DOES
ALIGNS WITH THEIR
COMPANY'S VALUES.

SOURCE: SHANE LOPEZ, SENIOR GALLUP SCIENTIST

IN A NATIONAL SURVEY OF FIRST-YEAR
COLLEGE STUDENTS, 76 PERCENT SAID THEY
ARE SEARCHING FOR MEANING AND PURPOSE
IN THEIR LIVES, AND 74 PERCENT SAID THEY
CHAT WITH THEIR FRIENDS ABOUT THE
MEANING OF LIFE.

SOURCE: "THE SPIRITUAL LIFE OF COLLEGE STUDENTS: A NATIONAL
STUDY OF COLLEGE STUDENTS' SEARCH FOR MEANING AND PURPOSE"

PEOPLE WITH A PURPOSE
IN LIFE REPORT LESS PAIN
AND ANXIETY, AND GREATER
HOPE AND OPTIMISM.

SOURCE: "THE ROLE OF EXISTENTIAL MEANING AS A BUFFER AGAINST STRESS"

"When we think about what makes us happy at work, I think most people might think, 'Oh, money or power,' but what we know about the workplace is we get even more motivation from a sense of purpose in our work, a sense that our work somehow matters in some greater context. When we exhibit altruism in our careers, when we help others, we actually help ourselves." —*Katya Andresen*

"An easy life is rarely meaningful and a meaningful life rarely easy."

—*Oliver North*

PEOPLE WHOSE LIVES HAVE PURPOSE AND MEANING TEND TO LIVE LONGER—AND BE HEALTHIER—THAN THOSE WHO DON'T.

SOURCE: "PURPOSE IN LIFE AS A PREDICTOR OF MORTALITY ACROSS ADULTHOOD"

Forty-two percent of small-business owners say the most rewarding part of owning a business is the freedom, while, surprisingly, only 7 percent say money.

SOURCE: WELLS FARGO/GALLUP SMALL BUSINESS INDEX

THE HAPPIEST CHILDREN BELIEVE THEIR LIVES HAVE MEANING AND VALUE, HAVE A STRONG SENSE OF PERSONAL WORTH, AND FOSTER QUALITY RELATIONSHIPS WITH OTHERS.

SOURCE: "SPIRITUALITY, RELIGIOUSNESS, AND HAPPINESS IN CHILDREN AGED 8–12 YEARS"

"[Having] meaning and purpose in life—I think it's everyone's birthright. Attaching yourself to something larger than yourself and dedicating yourself to it and bringing it about is, I think, completely controllable." —*Martin E.P. Seligman, Ph.D.*

"The purpose of life is to live it, to taste experience to the utmost, to reach out eagerly and without fear for newer and richer experience."

—Eleanor Roosevelt

Can living a meaningful life lessen our chances of developing Alzheimer's? Possibly, says one study, which reported that people with a greater sense of purpose have a lower risk of developing the debilitating disease.

SOURCE: "EFFECT OF A PURPOSE IN LIFE ON RISK OF INCIDENT ALZHEIMER DISEASE AND MILD COGNITIVE IMPAIRMENT IN COMMUNITY-DWELLING OLDER PERSONS"

photography credits

listed by page number

11. WAVEBREAKMEDIA

12. MONKEY BUSINESS IMAGES

15. SUKIYAKI

16. WAVEBREAKMEDIA

19. WAVEBREAKMEDIA

20. SYDA PRODUCTIONS

22. KUDLA

25. MONKEY BUSINESS IMAGES

26. HANNAMARIAH

29. EVGENY ATAMANENKO

30. GOODLUZ

34. WAVEBREAKMEDIA

36. SANDER VAN DER WERF

39. ANTONIODIAZ

40. AVAVA

43. OLESYA FEKETA

47. OLGA DANYLENKO

48. SUNNY STUDIO

50. RUBIKSCUBEFREAK

53. BARANQ

54. WAVEBREAKMEDIA

59. GOODLUZ

60. WAVEBREAKMEDIA

63. MONKEY BUSINESS IMAGES

64. ANDRESR

67. DRAGON IMAGES

68. OLESYA KUZNETSOVA

71. WAVEBREAKMEDIA

72. ALEXANDER RATHS

75. EFIRED

76. HALFPOINT

78. PRAISAENG

81. MONKEY BUSINESS IMAGES

82. WAVEBREAKMEDIA

85. HALFPOINT

89. BEBOY

90. OCSKAY BENCE

93. ANDRESR

94. BROCREATIVE

96. WARREN GOLDSWAIN

98. MONKEY BUSINESS IMAGES

101. AMMENTORP PHOTOGRAPHY

102. MONKEY BUSINESS IMAGES

105. MARYNA PLESHKUN

106. JAROMIR CHALABALA

109. ITSMEJUST

AT LIVE HAPPY, WE BELIEVE WHAT INSTINCT HAS LONG TOLD US AND NOW SCIENCE IS PROVING TO BE TRUE: Happiness exists within each person, waiting to be released and shared so it can magnify the happiness of others. It's a state of mind, an authentic way of being, a truth as individual and unique as each of us.

So we at Live Happy have a mission, not only to educate people on the journey of happiness but also to spread happiness to communities across the globe—one choice, one smile, one act of happiness at a time. We invite you to learn more about us by visiting **livehappy.com.**

livehappy™